BURNING THE PRAIRIE

BURNING THE PRAIRIE

Poems by John Reinhard

Minnesota Voices Project Number 31

NEW RIVERS PRESS 1988

Library of Congress Catalog Card Number: 88-60053
ISBN 0-89823-104-3
Typesetting: Peregrine Publications
Author photo by Sherida Bornfleth
Cover photo and photos for sections I and III by Larry Kanfer

Some of the poems in *Burning the Prairie* have previously appeared in the following publications:

Passages North
"The Fundamentalist Argues Against Darwin"; "Oh, Could Cheryl Ferguson Dangle"; "Spending the Night Beneath a Tree in Escanaba, Michigan"; "Blooding the Fawn"; "A Farewell to Conrad Sadorski"; "Michigan Wind for a Chinese Woman"; "When Fathers Speak for Daughters."

Abraxas
"Epiphany"; "Burning the Prairie."

Great River Review
"Kate Smith"; "Listening to the Birch Trees"; "For the Barmaid Unhappy with the Size of Her Breasts"; "A Poem for My Students."

Mankato Poetry Review
"Ernest Hemingway's Goat."

Raccoon
"The Talking of Hands"; "For Matthew: In Defense of Starlings"; "Keats at 50."

Sundog
"A Few Nights in Paducah."

Our thanks to the editors for permission to reprint here.

Burning the Prairie has been published with the aid of grants from the Jerome Foundation, the First Bank System Foundation, the United Arts Council (with funds provided in part by the McKnight Foundation), and the National Endowment for the Arts (with funds appropriated by the Congress of the United States).

New Rivers Press books are distributed by

The Talman Company   and   Bookslinger
150-5th Avenue   213 East 4th Street
New York, NY 10011   St. Paul, MN 55101

Burning the Prairie has been manufactured in the United States of America for New Rivers Press, Inc. (C.W. Truesdale, editor/publisher) 1602 Selby Avenue, St. Paul, MN 55104 in a first edition of 1,200 copies.

To the memory of my sister Laura
a painter of pictures

For my mother and father

CONTENTS

I. Riding the Edges of the Sky

II. Even So Long Ago as Now

III. Alive in Fire

I

Riding the Edges of the Sky

Kate Smith

"It's not over till the fat lady sings."

I liked her. She sang for all the less-than-lovely
ones. For anyone who's waited for the dark because
only then do we dare let the world see our light.
Her voice shone above an eternity of perfect noses.

Back in the 50s, for all the bad jokes,
I thought Kate Smith was sexy. I even had fantasies,
imagined being alone with her, putting my hand over
her mouth. Until I was eleven, I thought
this was the most intimate thing you could do
to another human being. Think about it.
Kate Smith in her prime and that voice
captured by you, for a moment, America huge
and singing in the palm of your hand.

The Fundamentalist Argues Against Darwin

Saying that human beings are more like frogs
than they are like monkeys anyhow.
You boo him, of course. But you wonder
about this — if maybe he's right. There
are times such as when you're making love
and a thick sound way back in your throat
crouches not unlike your body and you
repress it just as you repress at moments
this desire to jump. To see how high off
the ground you can escape, and maybe
how softly you might come down.
You've read of how the male frogs in spring
will screw coke bottles, each other, even
poisonous mushrooms; how these frogs share
with you this problem of distinctions. You
question whether Darwin ever listened
carefully enough to the story of the
frog that was changed into a man
by the kiss of a good woman.
By now you swear that the largest vein
in your arm is green. Your eyes shade
dangerously away from the blue you claim
is yours. Suddenly you are afraid
of ponds. Afraid. Of waking some night
to the sound of others, their knees to their chins,
all of them croaking Jesus in their sleep.

Grape Pickers

Everyone is out in
the vineyards of Texas Corners,
picking all the grapes they want
for jam or juice or early
winter wine.

She is forty-six, alone
in her row, just moved north
from Fellow's Dam
in Tennessee.
She is nearsighted like
that aunt so many of us have
who always marries the wrong man.

Sipping his morning beer,
Earl walks up, sets his bucket
down beneath her vine.
"Lovely day," she says,
as Earl nods and tosses a solitary
grape into his mouth.
Then he confides to her,
"Harleys ain't so much
bikes as they are projects."

She smiles and leans toward
Earl's chest, squinting
to read the white-lettered
message of his t-shirt:

> BIKERS ARE A
>   STRANGE BUNCH
> WHAT OTHERS CALL
>   PUSSY
> THEY CALL LUNCH

"Oh," she says
with a crack running through her
Fellow's-Dam-in-Tennessee voice.

Earl sips his beer
and grins at her.
She wonders if they will fall
in love. "You know," Earl says,
"I got mem'rized every
song Woody Guthrie ever wrote."

Then he plops another grape into
his mouth, picks up his empty
bucket, and walks
away, spitting a Concord
seed into the air, as far
as she can see.

The Ghost of Voltairine de Cleyre

She wished to become a famous anarchist
poet. Not surprisingly, her love life
was usually a mess.
—Page Smith, from *The Rise of Industrial America*

1.
There have been nights I've slept
with the thought that Amelia Earhart
would come to me and tell me
where it is a woman goes
when she must disappear. Or
that Eleanor Roosevelt would
suddenly be standing in a perfect
light, telling me all about the story
of Cinderella, the ashen girl
who made good. Or that Jeanne d'Arc
would appear, smoke in her eyes,
to tell the fury of a true vision.
To tell how pure the world
can be in its extremes. So how
do I explain this ghost of Voltairine
unwrapping herself from the sheet
she wore a century ago and spreading it
over me, dark for a moment, until
I feel her thigh nudging mine and hear her
asking me what it means at last
to be a modern man.

2.
Voltairine says the great discovery of the twentieth century is
the human mouth. I believe her. The way her mouth
communicates with every part of me, rolling each slowly
across her tongue. I have seen the sky in the same way
playing with certain clouds. When Voltairine's mouth is silent
she says, Now you talk to me. Tell me something
you would never expect me to believe.

3.

I want to grow closer to the sound
of my own voice which is many voices.
Voltairine says an old music involves
itself, so my left hand plucks out chords,
my right hand strums. But it's always
one hand after another. Voltairine says all men
have this gift. It is why men are better
at masturbation than at making love:
We are all one handed.

4.

A free woman according to Voltairine
knows many hands. Hands of women,
hands of men. The taste of her own
fingers. A woman never marries
for this is a closing off of hands.
A woman never drinks alcohol
for this is a numbing of hands.
A woman never prays for this
is a disclaiming of hands. Thus a woman
who clenches her fists knows much.

5.

I want to take her in some vague dance.
She moves away. Voltairine has quit poetry,
saying that no matter how hard she tries the rhymes
take over. Couplet after couplet. I put
my face to her neck and sense only
that her eyes are turning away from me.
She tells me there are certain moments like this
that listen in on the whole of our lives.
And what we hear will probably be
as simple as the sound of a mouth taking
shape, a breath about to be transformed.

6.
Figure this:
When I tell her I have a toothache
she says that teeth are phallic
symbols. So what's a smile become,
I wonder. I have taken to hiding bottles
throughout the house. Voltairine wants to assassinate
the President of the United States. To take
hostages. At times, we lie together.
On my ceiling I've pasted some glow-in-the-dark
moon and stars a friend has sent. Underneath
this simulation of sky we reach for one another
but don't touch. Voltairine says that
in her day, silly as it was, at least
they attached their wishes to the real thing.
I remind her that the only man she ever loved
drank poison. That the father of her only child
treated her like the thin sheet she wore
as she mesmerized the young men and women
of her time with talk of free love. Of a world
unrestrained. I remind her that the history
books describe her simply as the young and beautiful
anarchist, Voltairine de Cleyre, as though she can never
grow old, even one hundred years later, her long hair
braided like rope, and the bright synthetic
moon unleashing itself against her eyes.

When Fathers Speak for Daughters

As I see my daughter, she is soft
with fur. It is always twilight
when the boys call out her name,
boys who would run their fingers through her,
ride her off into the night where
I dream my daughter, her voice
a fine line between mother
and father, one day and another.

- - - - -

I wrote a man to tell him I loved his daughter
and wanted to elope with her. Maybe go north
to a small cabin by the big lake. He wrote back:
>   I wd. lock up my daughter—which one?—ere
>   I gave her hand (or any other part) to you (or
>   the likes of you), filthy of mind, unclean
>   of talon.   I'm serious.

- - - - -

When a woman exploded almost
in the stars, the reporters gathered
around her father, asked him about
what a father does when his daughter
disintegrates among the clouds.
As though only a mother's grief remains
unspoken, as though only a mother
might travel with a daughter
into places beyond words.

- - - - -

But what of the father who takes his daughter
as he would a wife. Maneuvers his body
and blood over hers. Says love is secrecy.
And when she becomes enough woman
to tell him, No, he jabs an awl into her belly,
bleeds her to a young death in the straw,
buries her in a field without trees
—nothing to keep the dust in its place.

- - - - -

I will have to tell my daughter that she
is on her own like all of us. Tell her
there is no longer any such thing as
protection. But in the always twilight
I will cradle my awkward arms, holding them
out to her as some slight shelter, father to daughter,
these arms no weapon, these hands no claim.

The Talking of Hands

You are in love for the first time. You are twelve.
Next to you is a deaf girl, maybe ten years old.
The two of you are on a train
easing its way through
the Cascade Mountains of Oregon.
You are so sure of this girl
you tell her everything. How
your voice is changing its shape.
How you are becoming something
remarkable. She smiles at you,
touches your arm. Later on,
in a darkening of trees she sleeps
on your shoulder. Gives to you
the soft whispers of her breath.
When she wakes up, you realize
you are over thirty years old.
This young girl says words to you that seem
out of shape, far away. Then
she starts talking to you with her hands.
You begin to understand the makings
of her language—where rain becomes
a drizzle of fingers and where, soon,
it will be a heavy enough rain
that she will show you how to make rivers
with your hands, your thumbs anchors
against the long, wild rush of water.

The Sign on Tom Lynch's Wall

An Irishman is never drunk as long as he can
hold onto one blade of grass and not fall off
the edge of the earth.

1.

Lynch is a mortician, who also happens to read
a lot of Yeats, writes a fine sonnet, and
by outliving the land commission of Ireland
has acquired a farm near the sea, a stretch
of ground whose name you might only sing
or imagine. I offer to work this land for him
but when he asks me what I'd plant, all
I can answer is "Sheep," and we leave it alone.
After about half a bottle of Jameson's
we reach a time for myth, the kind heavy
with whiskey and lies too small for keeping.
So with blades of grass between our fingers
and pieces of earth soft on our tongues, Tom
Lynch and I become the stuff of legend.

2.

Tom met a man in Ireland. A tiny man,
naturally, who sold locks of hair—death rod
and all that remained of the mistresses
of the Druids. Women who gave themselves freely
to trees. Pulled twigs from their thighs
and laughed long into the leaves.
So when Tom happened into this guy most certainly
on the right side of magic, Tom said,
"Look, I'm lonely. You have connections."
Tom gave the man a few dollars, a couple
of drinks, some saplings. In turn,
the man introduced Tom to a woman—
not red haired but young and attractive.
Before long, she and Tom were married.
They had several children and were happy

for a while. Then it all fell apart.
Divorce. Bad blood. Tom sent a lock
of her hair to the guy in Ireland, and
a note: "I have custody of the children;
stay on your side of the ocean." There
was no reply. Another shot of Jameson's.
Tom looks at me. "Marry someone young
and attractive, there's hell to pay.
Doesn't matter the color of her hair, or
how much magic she has behind her."

3.
When I was a boy—Tom listens now—
this doctor told me my heart
had a bad rhythm. I only wanted
to play basketball. I told the coach
this, whose response was
"I don't want anybody dropping
dead on the court while I'm coach."
For a couple of years I lived with that.
Wondering where the lost beats of my heart
went. Where I'd drop dead next.
Then I wanted to try out for baseball,
had another doctor put an ear close
to my heart. In fact, he put his head
almost through my ribs, listened
like Ulysses. Heard everything
the way he was supposed to.
What happened? Did this doctor
just have his own way of hearing
things? Tom answers, saying that Indians
waited for trains to ambush
by resting an ear against the tracks.
Incredibly, though, the slightest rain down
the line would throw them off, have them
thinking cavalry, Tom says.

4.
Lynch, like most undertakers, has a way
with punchlines for other people's stories.
Then he surprises me, tells a secret
about each body he's ever embalmed
or burned. Just before sticking a suction tube
into their gut or bagging them for the oven,
he presses his ear against the chest,
its skin cool like castle stone.
You actually listen for a heartbeat, Lynch?
Tom smiles, sips his whiskey. Cavalry,
he says. The goddamned cavalry.

5.
Many years ago, when America was the greenest
country in the world, the greatest tenor
in Dungarvin came over the ocean to recreate
Ireland in various bars along the eastern shore.
He brought a beautiful woman, a distant
cousin, to play concertina for him as he sang.
He loved her, looking right at her
whenever he sang anything particularly
sweet. The odds are that she loved him
too. Yet he could never tell her how he felt.
He waited for some mythical beast to come along
that might at least frighten her into love,
but the way it worked out, he lost
his voice, she lost her touch. They went
their sad and separate ways. They deserved
better. However, this is Tom Lynch's story;
the bottle is empty; and, in case you forgot,
Tom's most inspired relationship went bad. All
of this leads to unhappy endings for even
the best of stories. I've been known
to tell a few of these myself.

6.

When Lynch goes up to put his children to sleep
I head for home. Through the open window I
can hear that Tom's high and off-key
voice is lost in lullabye. Good night.
Good night. How can I fall from earth
when in my arms I hold these ones
I love. Good night. Good night.

7.

One time, Tom Lynch, I got so drunk
I sang in tune. This never happened
before or again. At least in front
of anybody. But this once I remember
some applause. The next morning
all of it had disappeared. Still,
for a moment I was crooning
to the colors of the earth, and the earth
chose not to look away, chose not
to shrug its shoulders when I said,
"Name a song. Listen. There I am."

Niobe Looks to North Dakota

Of her arms he was the hero and he sang . . .
This is how many of the ancient songs begin.
Some old man, usually blind, sings of the wars
that claimed his sons, transforms the fields
of blood into legend thick with tall and golden
grasses. All the while, Niobe weeps.
She weeps to form the seas and great rivers
of our earth. She weeps her way
through rocks and the hard bones of her children.

Driving north from Bismark you follow
a few wide turns of the Missouri.
Your life is a mess. A longing
to pull the sky close. Approaching
Minot you sense the missiles that lurk
in the wheat, ready to push the sky
even farther away from you. You fear
the absence of children. You fear
the loss of a child. You fear the end
of the world and only you survive.

Above Minot, Canadian geese form their peculiar vee
like an uncertain arrow. You drive
without direction, the Missouri now aimed
west to Montana. New rivers you find are small,
named mostly for Indian nations long dead.
You can imagine Niobe nearby, swelling
these creeks to overflowing. You drive on,
past silos pointed to the comets, toward
some horizon, the thinnest, most endless of lines.

Near the Stockyards

1.

Something is definitely wrong, you think,
as you watch nothing but wildlife programs
on the television. The 7th Annual Arthur Smith
King Mackerel Tournament from Myrtle Beach,
South Carolina. 8000 pounds of king
mackerel weighed in. That old angler, a local,
stares out at you. "Son, I feel
part of every fish that comes in here,"
he says, broken line trailing
from the hooks buried in his chin.

2.

A while back, you walked with a woman
and eyed the animals at the Omaha Zoo.
You saw a camel break loose. Saw a picture
of two elephants heavy in the act.
You stayed at a motel not far
from the stockyards. She was a woman
with uncommon hair, who talked
long and lyrically into the night.
You wanted to hear her. Actually,
you wanted to make love to her. At least
rub her to sleep, to a fine dream.
But she slept on her own. You wondered
how the camel avoided being hit by that train.
You wondered what noises the cattle
were making in their pens, wondered
whether you might, as usual, listen in.

3.

In the Wild Kingdom, the salmon are running.
A gauntlet of grizzly, wolf, fox,
and gull lines the river. To jump
high and lucky enough is a survival
of moment. The salmon flame red

for their death swim home, to where
the jaws of the males enlarge
for battle, to where the females
slap the gravel river bottom
with their tails, dorsals falling
and rising with the dropping
of eggs; the males at the last
with their milk, the fuse. Then
there is the famous dying. The body
finally succumbing to its bruise.

4.
If only men and women could figure out
a separate coupling of their own, maybe
you'd be better off. You think not,
then smile, imagining your fingers stroking
her breasts five minutes after she has left
your room. She may not even realize
how excited you are making her. You nibble
her flesh in air. Maybe you are happier
when you kiss the mouth of a woman
who has long since said good-bye.

For Matthew: In Defense of Starlings

Okay, I know what it's like
to want to kill them. I've held stones
like guns in my hand and felt there the weight
of a death without remorse.

Matthew, you're twelve years old. You live
surrounded by trees filled
with mourning doves, with birds blue
and gold that all sound like
really expensive music boxes
brought to America from thousands of miles
and hundreds of years away. So when
the starlings come along, your father
offers you a dollar for each one you shoot—
a dead starling is a beautiful song
from another bird, your father says.
For the starlings steal the nests
of the glamorous, drive them off
to places far from you; and then
the starlings even try to steal the songs
of the other birds, mimic notes
they've overheard on blue mornings.

If starlings were men, they would sing
in the shower. That is their lot. They would sneak
into the rooms of those they love, and
in the dark they'd touch the sleeping
shoulders they dare not caress in daylight.
They would be ridiculously shy, and walk
in empty fields where they would
imagine themselves as thieves
who stole trees from anybody
wealthy in wood.

I know that a dollar a bird
is big money. That when the starling

wheezes a pilfered song, it's not
a pretty thing. Yet you're a boy
still reaching for the sound
of his own voice. Think of that
when you hear the starling, inept
but confident. And when you want to hear
a prettier song, walk for a while.
If someone thinks you're lost,
that's all right. You'll know
you're headed to where the birds
are perfect.
       In the meantime,
you'll be able to say you looked the starling
in that small eye, and you listened
to each discordant note it struggled
to give you. You nodded. You let it live.

Epiphany

1.
The bus is thirty miles out of Dallas
when the chemical toilet malfunctions,
sending fumes up the aisle,
reminding me of Mr. Keller's cabin on the bay
and the old outhouse where I learned
the excesses of my own body
and threw squirming minnows
down that hole to see
if somehow they'd survive.

The man in the seat next to me
reaches for his overhead light
as if it's some star tilting favorably.
He says,
  Do you mind if I read
  Can I borrow your book
  I'm a big Rory Calhoun fan
  I tried pot once but it put me to sleep
  My wife left me
  My son's a pimp
  Those that walk with the Lord never need crutches
  I repossess cars for a living
  How do you feel about homosexuals?
The baby in the seat behind me
grabs my hair and begins to cry.
Her mother slaps her.

We are twenty hours from Denver.

2.
By Lubbock
my car repossessor has flown the bus
in search of a coupe.
We press on; the driver has his mind
on slow pick-ups, bright lights
oncoming, and north Texas
waitresses. Unable to sleep,
I imagine fat snakes all
along this highway's edges.
Diamond backed, looking
for apple trees and women denied,
they end up fleshed out,
their guts travelling through the treads
of overloaded semis headed for Cheyenne.

My fellow passengers dream.
Some of them snort and dribble
in the moments of their sleep.
        These are the ones dreaming about sex.
Some of them toss and turn
reaching for empty seats
or for themselves.
        These are the ones dreaming about love.
Some of them lie still like smoke
with smiles on their faces
and their hands folded prayerfully
across their bellies.
        These are the ones dreaming about death
        or rich food, or perhaps some place
        they were once before, that they can
        only come back to in their sleep.

I shut my eyes
but my mind fills with pictures of snakes
whose stomachs spill from their mouths

while their groins hurtle across highway 25,
highway 287, across hairless miles, long roads
to ride until Wyoming.

3.
The sun rises in the east.
And after three days without a drink,
after three days of buses
through Little Rock, Arkadelphia,
Hope, Texarkana, Sulphur
Springs, Dallas twice,
Waxahachie, Waco, Temple,
Lampasas, Leander,
Austin, Abeline, and
Sweetwater,
my bowels finally move in Amarillo
in a greasy spoon bathroom
where, in adjoining stalls,
men wearing Italian loafers
are blowing etudes intended for wind instruments
triumphantly out their assholes
while our fellow travellers
can be heard complaining
in the dining area
about cold toast and coffee
crisper than their bacon.

We are ten hours from Denver.

4.
I take my night's sleep in fifty minutes
across a north Texas morning.
I wake to a vision that is Oklahoma,
flat and endless as a Sunday sermon.
Where the sky and land reach no conclusion,

come not even to a minor understanding.
There are signs scattered
all along these roads.
"Are you looking for Jesus?"
they ask. And I laugh because
I was only looking for a place
to sleep and I ended up discovering
Oklahoma.
            There are riders immersed
in their *Redbooks* and *Newsweeks*,
and others with eyes looking out windows,
waiting for something to happen, somewhere.
If I were to tell them, "Look out the window,
folks — this is it!" they would nod,
and say, "Of course," and flip
their pages, and almost curse.
And they would wonder, how long, how long
to Denver.

Relocating the Elk

(for Stephen Dunning)

We lead them away from where
they've always been. In Montana
and Minnesota you can see
the long procession of elk.
We have told them there are new places
where fences can be safely jumped
and corn can be taken without cost.

When my grandfather passed on
some men from our town
dressed up in antlers
of elk, chanted over
the open casket,
tossed in a few berries and prayed. It remains
my fondest memory of death.

All along their journey, the elk
nuzzle each other, on
occasion probing with tongues
or horns. Noses in the air
for wolves or sweet flowers. Always
something carried in the wind.

Ear-tagged and light-hooved,
happier than most of us, they
hear us, follow our voices down
this long, strange road to Canaan.

Great Uncle Norvell Fast Is Dead

When death won out, Norvell was about 80.
He'd been married a long time to great aunt Kate.
At every family party, after the whiskey
Kate would say that her marriage succeeded
because, each morning, Norvell
would sit on the toilet first, to warm
the seat for her, for great aunt Kate.

Every year, we'd laugh, even though
we thought it was pretty strange. Every year,
Norvell would nod, sip his drink, and say,
"I defy anybody to tell me different:
It's every small gesture of love
that matters. And besides
Kate deserves a warm place to wait
for the everyday coming up of light."

But now Kate, already older than she wants
to be, must also deal with the unbroken chill
of waking. With the long cool night.

On the same day that Norvell Fast died
so, too, did a friend of mine. Out west
where the land is supposed to expand,
my friend stared into his thirtieth year,
into the sun he saw buried in the mountains,
and he decided that the next step
was too much, was enough.
So he cut himself away from his legs,
away until blood told him all he thought
he needed to know. He forgot
two children. A woman who loved
him. Forgot about a country
that would've waited for him.

At some point, memory fails many of us.
Maybe it even failed Norvell Fast.
But I doubt it. Even in death's face
I expect Norvell refused to claw
at the earth. More likely, he reached
for a drink, said, "I'm still good looking,
I'm still putting my arms around a remarkable
woman who will never stop calling out my name,
I'm riding the edges of the sky, and
I defy, I defy, I defy."

II

Even So Long Ago as Now

Listening to the Birch Trees

(for Tom Hennen)

Outside of the willow that weeps, the birch
is the only tree I can identify
with any confidence. I apologize
to oak and elm and maple
wherever they are. But I grew up
amid the birches, and I've been known
even now to strip away the thin bark
though I'm told this kills the tree,
that it can turn an entire forest of birches
into a field of bark, strings of trees
stretching out like cattle bones across
the prairie.
      The best thing about birch trees
is that they attract voices. So sometimes I walk
and listen in places where the birches gather.
I hear Miss Gilhoulie, my kindergarten teacher,
still telling me—because I would not remove
my Davy Crockett cap—to sit behind the piano
where the music hides and small boys fade away
just like old soldiers. I can hear my grandmother
who says her only regret is that
she doesn't think my grandfather knew how much
she loved him. That when she heard his voice on the phone
it still thrilled her. That when she saw him
walking toward her with his footballer's body
she quivered inside—fifty years, she says, and she shook
with love. I find myself straining in hope that I too
might hear my grandfather's voice, that at least his smoke
might swirl noisily through the branches and it might
say that love can move beyond words and be understood.

Then I hear the voice of a young woman. She has memorized
the names of all the rivers of the world. She is not afraid
of talking back to birches. I would like to say to her

something beautiful and true — to imitate for her the sounds of birch, the plaintive whispers of the leaves in the raw wind, the long trees so sweet in their unravelling.

Not Letting Go of Lauren Bacall

My grandfather loved her. Maybe
it was the voice like bourbon, the walk
that tightened up your trousers. Maybe
he saw himself as Bogart, the hat
always low on the forehead and the eyes
in shadow. My grandmother learned
to live with the fact that her husband
was really in love with Lauren Bacall.
My grandmother raised five children, taught
at the Garfield School, drank whiskey
in the afternoons, and loved her man.

Just a few years before he died
of a disease nobody could figure out,
my grandfather was watching some talk show
and, all of a sudden, there she was.
Lauren Bacall. A little weathered perhaps
but still beautiful in the way that was
hers. In less than ten minutes
he found out her real name was Betty
Perske, her famous "look" was actually
just a case of nerves, and worst of all she was
a Jew. My grandfather turned off
the television. Never spoke her name
again. When she turned up later
in some interview or even the old films
he simply muttered "Jew" and left
whatever room he was in. I never knew
where he went to, what language
he spoke to himself. All I knew was
that he'd let go of Lauren Bacall
and that he would not take her back.

My grandfather died a day-by-day
kind of death. As though the spirit
waded its way cautiously into deep water.

33

The words went first. Then the hands.
Then the eyes. At the funeral, the priest
used my grandfather as a metaphor
for the human condition, for the wasting
away, and said religion was the answer.
I could've killed that son of a bitch, death
so close as it was. At least I could've
taken him down to the old theatre in town
and put him in the front row and shown him
Lauren Bacall's first movie. The one
where she says, "If you want me, just whistle;
you know how to whistle, don't you? You just
put your lips together and blow." The priest
might've said, Just put your hands together
and pray. But my grandfather needed something more
as he travelled toward death. Something more certain.

Father, whistle to God and you might make
music. But whistle to Lauren Bacall
and you make love. Whistle in her direction
and you have never made a sound so sure.

Years of the Bear

Black bears walk along
sand ledges of the great lake.
It's been said that if
you rip open their stomachs
you will find the remnants
of the lost children of the north.
The ones who wandered off
to run their hands along the birches
and never returned.

To survive the age of twenty-seven
I rode the humped backs of the bears
and told myself,
"Wait until thirty,"
and stroked the thick, black fur.
"Wait until thirty
and a woman will save you."

In lawn chairs on lake front
old men sit and grab
for their hearts when bears
pass close. They dream
of shooting light
into dark. They think
about the warmth
of caves and paws
heavy on bear wives.

I hesitate someplace
where these old men sing
loud songs of unknowing,
not savage memories of love.
They fill jars with their honeyed songs.
They fill shelves and shelves with jars.

They lick their fingers.
They are hungry for the happiness of bears.

Oh, Could Cheryl Ferguson Dangle

In the Lincoln School playground in 1963
she was a vision hanging
from the monkey bars
and making faces at me as I watched
while a perverse wind
played with her skirt.

To show my affection for her
I threw small pebbles at her open mouth.
She swallowed one
and then dribbled down her chin
with uncommon grace for 1963
and the fifth grade.

Most people
who sew the past together with rough thread
stick a needle in 1963
and run the thread through the fragments
of Kennedy and November,
wrapping the days in black sheets
and laying them perfumed into the ground.

But for me
1963 is white-socked and red-cheeked
as Cheryl Ferguson dangles
in the Lincoln School playground,
sticking out her tongue like candy,
as a slick, nasty
wind plays strange, wonderful
games with the pleats in her skirt.

What Centerfield Used to Mean to the Yankees

A few of the farmers in Graceville
will sit in the old hotel and talk
for hours about how the thighs
of the girls from Big Stone County
used to be spectacular before
women lost their sense of direction.
Then the conversation will turn
to Vince Lombardi leaving Green Bay
for Washington, D.C.; to Mickey Mantle
retiring, finally, because of bum knees.

Mickey Mantle was my first hero.
I read his biography and rooted
for the Yankees right about the time
the trains stopped running
through our town. Once,
my father drove me down to Detroit
so I could see the Mick, but
it was Berra who hit the grand slam
and Mantle who didn't
run out a grounder to short.

Most everything these days returns
to some specific face
or name or sense of loss.
Back in the Graceville Hotel
it's beers all the way around
while one of the farmers goes over
to this young overweight blonde
at the magazine rack. They talk
for a long time; tell each other
stories—where she's Marilyn Monroe
and he's her Joe DiMaggio
with his trademark always up
and his hand
pounding the mitt.

The Killer in Minneapolis Woods, 1961

Wendy always knew.
"He slept there
where the tin cans are stacked.
They mark a grave,
probably."

We used to walk in the woods
most every day that summer —
Wendy, Debby,
Brian Larson, and I.
Through the graveyard
almost lost in ferns
we'd walk and look
on stones for dates
not yet worn away
of those who had died young.
We found the killer
in each charred piece of wood,
in every hollowed-out stump,
in every leaf that was disturbed,
in each unnatural indentation of ground.

Wendy always told his story:
"He kills small children,
cuts them up,
feeds their pieces to the fishes."

And so we'd walk each day
on old paths
underneath the maples.
When someone crapped in the bushes
and left it for the winter
Wendy always said it was the killer's.
Brian Larson said it was his brother Ricky's.
Debby said it probably belonged to a bear.

It took ten minutes to walk
from one end of Minneapolis Woods
to the other.
Yet the killer evaded us
and we escaped him,
except for dead fires
and the hints of graves.
Amazing that somehow
at night unnoticed
he danced with the Indians
until the moon peaked
and then he'd steal some hapless
child
to slice to bits.
But I believed in him.
Maybe every child needs
some killer to run from,
some nightmare to dream.

Maybe I was just crazy

The killer was never seen,
never captured.
Wendy said some hungry deer
ate him while he slept.
Debby said it was a bear.
Brian Larson said
his brother Ricky had nothing
to do with it,
he was just a kid who liked to crap in the bushes.

Spending the Night Beneath a Tree
in Escanaba, Michigan

1.
The wind knows
exactly
where this man's spirit
ends
and his body takes command.

2.
At Bay de Noc
the rabbits come out at night
and bounce across the grass.

The moon is full and round
and circles the noises of the dark
as if searching out
some undiscovered other.

My ass is cold
as my newspaper blanket
blows toward the woods.
And I've discovered
I have a fear of rabbits
who come out
at night

and play.

Blooding the Fawn

1.
The fawns die first,
necks snapping when young
mouths reach for a leaf
or piece of greenery
too far away.

In their death they lie
waiting for men like me
to come and take
the young bodies in our arms,
to bloody our faces
and whisper a love to these
bones scattered like arrowheads
all the way to Ironwood.

2.
On our way to her town, we stop
at Pooches Bar which overlooks
a frozen Garfield Lake
where an old man and a boy walk
on ice I hear cracking
at their every step.

We drink pitchers of Miller Beer.
We play George Jones songs
on the jukebox because we like
how sadly he can sing.

While driving here, we passed
Sid Murphy's Fine Hog Farm
and the pigs were singing, too,
in mournful tones,

"It's just the same ole me
Lovin' the same sweet you . . . "

Antlers hang above
the bathroom doors;
she hesitates there,
then comes back and asks me,
"Am I a buck or a doe?"

Later, we manage the curves
to her parents' house,
to where her mother tries to sleep
and her father eyes us
as though he knows we were
listening to George Jones singing
"It's just the same ole me,"
as though he knows I told his daughter
she was a buck
and that she almost believed me,
as though he knows I crept like a thief
into the dark room of his daughter, this woman,
and that I did not leave alone.

3.
In her winter town mostly
there is just the Congregational Church
and the cemetery stones that kneel
down into the woods of a slight valley.
The only movie theatre closed.
The one bar, Jan and Don's,
doesn't open until noon.

The wind, colder than we thought
it was, numbs her hand
in mine. Pockets would be warmer,
but we let our fingers freeze
together, and a light snow is driven
along a horizontal line
so that it never seems to touch
the ground.

We cut behind Kayle's Korner Store,
the quickest way home.
By the back door,
in the parking lot empty of cars,
there is a severed head
lying wide-eyed and bloody.
Its long tongue hangs.
Two horns curl around its skull.
We stare a few seconds,
wondering if it's antelope or
mountain deer, buck or doe
but not knowing, and we run,
we who were raised among omens.

4.
A few days later,
we spend what will be
our last night together
in a motel on Washtenaw Avenue where
the trucks run heavy.
We watch a sort of erotic
movie on the cable television.
Afterward, she hides beneath the sheets
and says to me, "You're the sexiest
man I've ever met."

Since neither of us is drunk, I figure
we're in love like
Gary Cooper and Merle Oberon.
What I grew up believing in.

It's fantastic at times what we
believe. How we know
something exists even when
we can do no more than
brush our fingertips against it

43

on only the most extraordinary
of days. How we know.

What we don't know is that
soon her mother will die,
that a heart no one doubted
will fail. That many hearts
will fail. That there is no knowing
how the child in the belly
of my brother's wife will die
in their happinesss, will die
after seven months and leave marks
where it scraped and kicked
to know something of this life.
How two lovers — even if
they might survive the shudders
of trucks — will not survive
each other's sadness. How the blood
of the fawn's heart, smeared
across the faces that believe, will fail
like potions or chants
or hands rubbed across the skulls of saints.

5.
Of course, what this comes back to
is a story. My uncle, a man filled
with stories, told me
If you ever touch a fawn
just as it dies, its soul will travel
through your fingers, and if you
then rub the blood from its
still-beating heart across your face
your love life will be charmed.

He is my favorite uncle, a quarter Chippewa,
and he told me this before

his wife left him, so I believed the story,
and probably still believe it,
the fawn reaching with its red
mouth for the greenery, reaching,
so close, for the unknowing.

A Farewell to Conrad Sadorski

There is just one tree
on Groesbeck Highway. But
you found it one drunken
night a month ago and wrapped
your soul around it. All of us
must one night face alone our own
fatal crashing, but yours could've been
avoided if you'd only called a cab.

Back in 1981, at our class reunion,
we had a few drinks together.
It was pleasant enough. And I was glad
you never asked me what I remember
most about you. That was back
in eleventh grade, when we were
playing ping pong in your basement.
Your mother was unloading clothes
from the Maytag. She was not
a particularly attractive woman,
but she was wearing that day
a loose-fitting robe and whenever
she leaned over to fold some sheets
her breasts swayed like a lullabye
and I thought that lady lovely.

When Greg Zane fell from a helicopter
to his military death, I remembered the smile
of his girlfriend. When Chris Fetzer
died of cancer, I thought about the leather
jacket he so uncomfortably wore.

Conrad, forgive me if you can,
but I can't forget your mother's breasts
on what was probably the last day I ever
really looked you in the eye.

Deciding to Ignore Death

Back home in Sault Ste. Marie, there's nobody
left to die. Back home the whorehouse madam
pays her taxes, her girls do not sparkle
their way into the river, and the tourists stay forever.

This is where I grew up. There was a big house
on Young Street. In our basement
was an underground passage that wound
beneath the river into Canada, but
I stayed where I was, played in the coal bin,
sang very quietly, and became
the blond boy with the black tongue.

I used to play sometimes
with a neighborhood girl who'd ask
about the tunnel into Canada. Who'd say
she knew of places where the waterfalls
froze in winter. I'd take her down
to the basement where we'd roll together
on the cold floor, then try to shake the dust
off one another. What gravity and hands
could not displace, we'd lick away,
and then we'd kiss,
black mouths hard together.

Sault Ste. Marie, Michigan, is the only town
in the world where every furnace still burns
coal. I have come a long way from there.
But even so long ago as now I dream
of singing my black-tongued songs, of being
with a girl who so easily shakes
the dust away, who tells me of a place
where the water freezes as it falls.

A Few Nights in Paducah

And the almighty God will judge every man
according to his lights.

I read that somewhere before
I came to this river town on the Ohio
and the Tennessee, to be with a woman
who, I'm afraid, will love me for my moment
then let me go.

Every man according to his lights.

Alben W. Barkley lived in Paducah
and the locals have thanked the memory
of the old Senator, Mr. Truman's Vice President,
by patching up his house for the tourists to see.

But the lady and I are holed up
at a Holiday Inn.
She calls me Bambi;
I call her Thumper.
Such is the condition of romance
in the terminal stages of our century.

So we leave Alben W. Barkley to his history,
to the ghosts of two rivers.
We chose this town as a place
where two people could love
and maybe even drink beers
with some farmers from Eddyville.
A place where barges, their lights low,
slide along brown currents at night,
and we can see it all from our window
almost high above Paducah,
a regular Paris of the Ohio.

Michigan Wind for a Chinese Woman

(for Danny)

My brother and I sit on a bench
in some Michigan town.
He is eight years old,
blond as Kansas,
my almost son.

As a Chinese woman approaches
he farts, loud
like a fat priest rising
from a long kneel.

The Chinese woman walks by us,
no change of face.

I pass my brother my sternest look,
my father's eye.

"Maybe she doesn't speak English," he says,

and we laugh.

Pilgrimage

(for Jim Harrison)

1.
Sometimes it seems the world lies
just across the edges of this
bridge. Edges I've always been
afraid to look beyond. A fear,
I tell myself, of heights
as our truck rises above
the old fort and its history
of massacre; as we eye
the dusk, its blood light balanced
by the dark weight of island to the east.

I was born sixty miles straight ahead, past
Castle Rock, the Mystery Spot,
Pickford, past Trout Lake
and countless places best known
as towns left behind.
All of us from the country north
of Mackinac, no matter
how small our claim, hold to the whole
of the land from Drummond Island
to Little Girls' Point. And whenever
I cross the Straits, going north,
I imagine that feeling
of Peary returning from his conquest
of ice; of the poet Max Jacob rising
from his ashes to stand
on a bridge that safely bears
his name from one shore to another.

2.
I was raised to believe
that every woman was
the color of snow,

that every path through fir
trees, notched carefully, led
somewhere in particular.

We camp in a ten-dollar-a-week tent
on a section of those dunes
which frame Lake Michigan.
Even in early May, the winter's skeleton
can sometimes scrape its bleached
bones along this sand. But not
tonight. A mild south wind, the darkness
whispers. Jill is drinking Yukon Jack;
we talk about the one-eyed prophet
we travel for, and wonder
at our losses. She passes
the bottle to me, and says,
"Somebody once told me that when I cry I look Chinese."

And we dream this night the same
of dreams. Of Confucius
contemplating a porcelain tear
on the cheek of his mistress; contemplating
a wall that must be built,
that will be intended
to protect, but will serve only
to contain; contemplating that same
tear solid against the cheek
of a woman dreaming on sand just east of Manistique.

3.
How lovely it was when
the young girls lay their simple
bodies as angels to melt
against the small hills of my white country.

Thigh deep in a stream unknown

to us and to our maps which speak
of Waiska, Milakokia, Bear,
Nawakwa, Two Hearted, we fish
for rainbow though we
have no idea of runs or
seasons, lures or lines.
The woman's steadier than I am,
less nervous away from land.
I've never caught anything
larger than a timid perch. Nothing
I couldn't wrap my hand around.
I've been told that here it's different,
that to lift the fish from the net you must
insert fingers into the pink slit
of its breath. I wonder whether
this will be soft or rough
with bones, whether it will
come alive and thrash or simply
die at my touch. I crave a drink
and find myself smiling at a woman
who's serious in the direction
of her river. We are two people
who lost all we thought that mattered.
I look to her. "You're tangling your line,
again," she tells me, and I reel it in.

4.
From highway 77, near the Fox River
and Seney, we notice a tepee
abandoned on its bank
and we remember our friend
Don Rice, how he may have been
closest to his journeys. The way
he moved from one point to another
with the precision of a flea.
Just before the tumor in his head

exploded, he built a tepee
on the Huron, became known
as the Hermit of his town;
finally, he lay down quietly there,
held fast by the careful arms of the earth.

5.
Jill and I drive north to Grand Marais
with rainbow trout and Tennessee
whiskey for the one-eyed prophet
who we hope will share
this bottle, will share these trout
we bought at a store
a few miles south of town.

Someone told us he picks
his teeth with wolf bone. Lost
his eye to the broken edge
of a tossed whiskey glass, said
someone else. Indian legend has it
You should always trust a man
who is able to see both light
and dark at the same time.

But after drinking Drewery's
at every bar in Grand Marais, we are
nowhere. The bartenders
put us down as tourists: "One-eyed man?
Never seen him here," they tell us,
and one old woman says she thinks
he's gone to Hollywood, that he remains
a destination. We polish off
his whiskey later, toss his fish
along the roadside for the bears.

That night, as Jill reads *Volpone*
by kerosene light, the lost
dogs of farmers howl. I fall into the tent,
ripping a hole through which
the mosquitoes invade our designs,
where I lean toward my snow angels again
as they flap their red stubs in hopes of heaven.

Philip Freneau Comes Home in the Cold

Even when you're falling down drunk, Revolution
is the human condition. What you break away from
that counts. Thus the lost cause beckons like
the snow bank where you rest, hoping that
you didn't leave the tavern earlier than was right.

A long time ago, this was a place for rolling around
with some radical who warmed her hand in your pocket
while you talked of honey suckle and fires. Later,
a place for pissing big as if the Declaration
were a high drift and you were John Hancock, himself.

You don't know what happened to the radical. Usually,
she married land and money, and then eventually
found God. You have a knack for driving women
toward God. And somewhere along the way
your bold signature shrivelled into slush.

It has become a new century; one is always giving way
to another. In a night darker than most you were lost
for awhile. But now what you will not know merges
with what you believe and what you dream. In a sea
white and frigid as the wings of angels you are floating.

III

Alive in Fire

Keats at 50

When all the beautiful young women come
up to you after the reading and tell you,
This was that lovely moment in my life,
they are probably not lying. So let them lie
beside you, pretend that moment
a little longer, imagine you more
than what you know you are.

A famous writer, after drinking heavily
in the afternoon, once said to you,
Do it all before you're 50,
which is the best advice you've ever had.
You look over your shoulder, see poems
scattered like so much litter
in the park, like the wreckage of your family,
their early deaths shadowing each tentative step
you take. What you'd give to be younger
— 35, let's say — still able to see the morning
as colonnades of light, and if you wanted
to shinny up one of these all the way
to the roof of the world, you'd have the time,
the strength, the tenacity to climb,
to do more than just hang on.

When all the beautiful women come
to let you be the words of their day,
you think back to the few you loved.
The ones you saw as gusts of wind
to riffle your hair. Too late
you see yourself the sail to hold them,
to let them carry you away.

So now, as some woman with Keats
in her eyes, with Keats nibbling her ears,
asks you of her future and what you'd share
about the poetry inside of you and her,
Die young, you're tempted to tell her, almost
believing yourself, almost falling
for the sound of your own voice.

Daddy D. Rewrites the Sky

1.
Son, he says, I just figured out
what growing old means: What you want
to get big, shrinks; and what you hope
will shrink, gets absolutely huge.

Even so, every once in a while, he slouches his way
to the outfield, and I hit him fly balls.
Hit 'em deep. All my life
I've looked to hit just one ball over
the fence. Daddy D. sticks up
his glove. Always. Flags down another one.

Babe, he says, hitting the homer's easy.
It's circling the bases that's tough.

2.
Sometimes, Daddy D. stands out there
in left field and tilts his head up
until the twilight gathers him in.
It's as though if he's patient enough
the moon will drop right out of the sky
and into his glove. Then, the right arm
that wrapped itself around Carla
Shransky in 1943 and told him
Man, this is heaven, that same
right arm will arc the moon
into a heaven all its own, into
a different arrangement of stars.

Champ, he says, when I was a kid
we couldn't afford the luxuries, so
to give the arm a workout we'd toss
cow turds into the sky. We'd pretend
they never came down, that they'd catch
the perfect high wind and fly

forever. We figured, why give them back
to the ground when the sky would take them in.

3.

Daddy D. is troubled. One of his daughters
has moved to Timbuktu. The other
—this gets worse—has moved to Iowa,
married a man who renames the parts
of animals.
        Did I ever tell you, he says,
how beautiful daughters are when
they're about six months old? After that
though their beauty's a constant, though
you always love them, you get scared
because you see them discovering you are not
the only man who is trying to hold
heaven in his arms.

4.

At some point, most of us see the moon
reflected on water, and we want to dive
in. To feel the moon against our fingers.
This happened to a friend of mine
up near Duluth, Daddy D.'s hometown.
My friend decided that his own story
was nothing more than an ending—the moon
on water—so he wrote it down.

Hey, Babe, says Daddy D., if you want to catch
the moon, you gotta look up. And he points
to something high above Duluth. Spit in your glove,
he says, and don't get fooled by shadows. He points
to where on certain nights I swear I see
the moon in places I never saw before.
Where the stars look spontaneous as sparks
and the whole sky verges on fire.

In the Land of the White Rat

It starts with me in a room
in a library. I am reading
a story you've heard before
when a young woman walks in
stroking the white rat perched
on her shoulder. She says,
"Didn't there used to be a poem
on this wall?" I shrug
my shoulders. The rat
shrugs its shoulders too.
"Too bad. It was a poem
I liked." She walks away
still stroking the white rat.
This is where the poet
secks connections. He wants to say
she will whistle Homeric hymns
all the way back to a grass hut
at the edge of a prairie river
where the rat will be transformed
into a young Gregory Peck; that the woman
has moonlight in her veins; that
the secret of happiness is hidden
in the poem she says was
on the wall. But what I see is
the white rat's
tail long
and pink down her back.
It is not unlike a thin braid of hair
that you have reached for in the dark
so you might twirl it between
your fingers, move it ever
so quickly across your tongue.

The Middle of Winter

There's no dealing with the lack
of conclusions. You come home
to her and try to conceal
yourself in her body. Something
explodes. You dream Nagasaki
at times. Sleep with survivors
who call you a name you've not
heard before. Touch you in
places you did not know were there.
- - - - -
I have caught her
drinking alone at night
when I came to call.
I wanted love. We
ended up watching television.
Tried not to wake
her children. Tried not to
shake any leaves from the trees.
On T.V. a faith healer from Ohio
cured a leg cramp through prayer.
- - - - -
The problem is simple:
You never let go
of your dead. Their scent
stays with you, lingers
in the space left
behind any lovely face
you pass on the street
that turns your head and leaves
you sniffing the air for perfume.
- - - - -
She falls down in front of the bar
not far from the river walk
where you first kissed her.
She's drunk. A stranger
helps her up, takes her home.

He changes her name, the way
she moves. You are alone
where the river lies
with its eyes waiting
to be closed. You sing
Stephen Foster songs. Watch
for boats to come along
that you might name after women.

- - - - -

He looks through
Her eyes
He has no idea
What to say
Love o love
Cunt he tells her
He feels something
Slam against his face
He thinks
It's a door

- - - - -

Yours is a world of Russian heroines trapped
in unfinished tragic novels. Their names
will always escape you. The soft
music will always be in the background.
You will never know more than what
you wanted to say to someone who was
gone before you could open your mouth.
Your tongue grows thick with stories
never told and light never promised.
You long for a woman who will
slap your face and shake loose
the words you've been waiting to let go.

To Believe in Princes

The crux of it, she says,
is that there aren't any more
Princes. That it is no longer safe
to fall recklessly in love.

I wonder what kind of voice
a Prince would have on the prairie
in the 1980s. How much
that voice would tremble. How
like a barn owl he might sound
when the sun at last settled
down beyond the Red River.

Celibacy, she says, is the one
solution. I want to disagree.
I want her to believe in Princes.
But this is the week the Russian fleet
is on maneuvers, preparing
for the possibilities of thermonuclear
war, and Merle Haggard
is still singing about the futility
of love and the wonders of drink.

    Somewhere, there is a Prince
down on his luck. Like all of us
he dreams of magic and comfortable
shadows he might stretch his skin against.
He cannot come to terms
with the out-of-tune piano
that constantly plays what sounds
like Brahms. With the old Hungarian
from the factory who tells stories
that never have endings.
And, mostly, with the absence of a girl
who would fasten herself to him like the rain.

    Meanwhile, back on the prairie,
The crux of it, she says . . .

Ernest Hemingway's Goat

We could feel alone when we were
together, alone against the others. It
has only happened to me once like that.
　　　　　—from *A Farewell to Arms*

He really did have one. Met it
in Cuba. Brought it back
to Idaho when Fidel took
over. The goat and Ernie
talked often. About how love
and sentences shared a certain
terseness. "Goat," Ernie would
say, "it's a tough fucking world."
"Yeah, tough," Ernie always
heard the goat say back.

Sometimes in Idaho the sun
would take a long time
in setting. Ernie and the goat
would sit and watch.
On the prettiest nights
they'd try to figure out
different ways to describe
the brilliant redness
of the sky. "Like blood,"
Ernie said. "Like an
apple," said the goat.

Then it happened that Ernie
became the color of the sky.
The goat watched as
the horizon filled with
theories about the color red.
But the goat just regretted
the loss of the hand that scratched
and stroked the long back.
The hand that fed to goat
one shiny apple after another.

A Distance

These sad faces I draw lately.
I say to them, Smile. Whisper to me.
But they edge always toward this
sorrow, to this strange grace.
At times, I bring their cheekbones
close to mine, wonder what would happen
curve to curve, flint to stone.

How is it the prairie provides
for some of us a distance
between ourselves and death
and love. A perfect grey country.

Sometimes, I stretch my sad faces
across the fields. I tell the farmers,
This will keep away the birds and evil
spirits . . . This is also my way
of explaining that night you found me,
my face to the ground, the bone
of my cheek turning hard into the earth.

Easter 1987

No one believes that to die
is beautiful, that after the hard pain
of the last unsaid word I am swept
in a calm out from shore
and hang in the silence of millions. . . .
        —Philip Levine, from "Belief"

1.
In silence, each small world ends. One word
dies into another as though death itself
holds together with its shadows
every sentence that is ours. My sister
on this morning has become the silence
in our father's voice, the break between
words tolling louder than bells.

This is supposed to be the day when
the dead come back, and across the street
the Episcopalians are alive with song,
emerging from their singing garbed
in rainbow. This is the day
when paths are cleared
and the holes in the roof
where souls shot up to ether
are mended.

I've been told that Christ died
for all of us, but that he was resurrected
for the benefit of the select.
The ones who knew the chants
and the proper angle of the eye
upward.
        I remember my sister tilting her head,
trying to find out where the light should shine
on whatever face she'd conjure up. And then as
she'd paint in oils and pastels that face would
become her face, become the creator.

On Monday, death itself returns.
What is dead is irretrievable.
The Episcopalians keep their mouths shut.
The bright colors move back to the sky,
to the other side of rain.

On Monday, my father and I pick up the possessions
of blood. A faded picture on a card.
A note addressed "To whom it may concern"
because to announce death is to talk to everyone.
A cord used to shut away the breath, the breath
that lovers share with one other, that they
use in the sharing of names and skins.

The breath that others transform into the long
wailing of loss, of being, of knowing
that to embrace the air is everything.

2.
We have known for a long time
that, on occasion, light flickers
before our eyes, and then is lost
forever.
        Two days after
Easter Sunday, I scatter your ashes
on the banks of the Yuba River,
in the foothills of the Sierra Mountains,
trout fisherman, on the other side of the rocks,
reaching out to the water. This was a place
where you would often come and sit,
sometimes to sketch the points
where water blistered to white
like misery beneath the skin
of the earth.
        Two days after
Easter Sunday, I stare at a horizon

scattered by the hills. I say the other side
of grief is love. I argue this
to myself and to the wind
where I leave you. You who said
that being an artist means not being afraid.
Means painting faces with eyes that look
straight ahead. But you left behind
paintings with unfinished faces, with eyes crossed
or unfocused as if they might see what you
could not, as if they might know the value of fear.

3.
I would like to think that this spot by the river
is one where sometimes couples sneak to lie down
and see how green this country is where they climb
into each other's arms, how white and blue
this river is that cools their thirst, that
washes away the dust that is not theirs.

4.
Today, I took some of your paintings
to have them framed in wood,
encased in fine glass. Paintings
of mothers and daughters. Paintings
of the little girl you still could remember
yourself to be. A sketch of the river,
the covered bridge, the steep and rocky place
where I released you like a seed
as if you'd grow again
out of the earth, rise toward these words,
this fragile poetry,
that I give you, only now
too late for even the faintest of good-byes.

Burning the Prairie

This fire restores life, the farmer tells you.
A torch to the grasses and out of the black
stubble eventually a better earth.

You imagine the whole of the Dakotas
aflame. Imagine also something burned away
inside of you—call it love if you want

or a certain curiosity. Imagine
it reemerging from a dark field
as if a moment of Christ in everyone,

even you, the nonbeliever,
all of you suddenly white
and alive, alive in fire.

Easter 1985

72

For the Barmaid
Unhappy with the Size of Her Breasts

She brings you a beer and sad eyes
that she says are bigger than . . . she looks
down. This is a slow night in bars
across America. Every husband has gone
home to his wife. So she sits with you.
Calls you sensitive. Complains that
her nipples feel too close to the rest
of her body, that she wants some space.
This part of her out front of everything else.

You figure a story here won't hurt, and tell her
you're just lately a farmer who's sown
his first field of oats, driven his first
antique John Deere tractor. Tell her
these oats are already rising, and all
the old Norwegians, snoose trickling
from their mouths, look
at the field and you and then
say, "Take pictures," as though no one
will believe this, how your rows waver
and stray from expected lines.
Even the birds stay away.

At this point, the barmaid buttons
the top of her blouse. Seems close
to tears. You keep going.

Tell her that you like your rows for all
their unevenness. And when aerial
photographs are taken, your field
will become famous in agricultural offices
all over the midwest. Before long,
the old farmers will be back, their chins
clean, to see exactly how it was
you planted. The moral of this,

you tell the barmaid, is that
what is ours is good. That you
have sown your oats and they
are lovely, wherever they lie.
That her breasts are lovely as well
and that size only matters in silhouettes.
At this she smiles. It is the sort of smile
you have skidded over icy roads to reach. It is
as though her entire body curves upward.

Almost Leaving Minnesota

From here, everything leans south.
The wind, the river. The skirts
women's legs drift into when
the weather's right. All of us
spit south, which is why
Iowa is so flat
and its corn so golden.

Right now the fields of Stevens
County are too muddy for tractors.
Crows mold themselves to the rain,
wait for seed. One farmer walks
into his field, sinks out of sight
through the dark song of this earth
that no longer bears his weight.

The last time I tried to leave,
near Taylors Falls I saw two horses
coupling in the sweet grasses.
Watched the awkward tenderness
in the loving. Spring, yes,
in their blood, but winter
still fresh in the hooves.

It is almost time to try to leave
again. To open up our hands
together.
      Not long ago, at a death
in a small Minnesota town
I sat silently while a basement
full of Lutherans sang out
"How Great Thou Art,"

and though I would not join them,
though I would not betray what I
do not believe, I was moved
by their conviction and
their noise. Moved by their
sad joy. By their belief
in the power of good-bye.

The Man in the Window

(to Francois Truffaut)

1.

Sometimes, I can see my life
as one of those quiet foreign films
where two people are always
falling in love in the rain.
It is Paris, of course. Not quite
dark. Music singing from the gutters.
Trains are close by. The lovers
take a long walk down a street
filled with famous scenes.
They stop to stare into the window
of an exclusive shop, where the man
notices only himself reflecting back.
The woman, obviously, is on one of the trains.
(She will marry a guy who
used to hit her and works now
in a Mexican restaurant. After
two years of marriage, he will begin
to hit her again. He will get fat, too.
She will never leave him.) Meanwhile,
the exclusive shop in Paris
with the man in the window
becomes a boarded-up department store
in downtown Detroit. A man looks into
the wood for some semblance of a face.

2.

How I wish the world could be
the colors of our dreams, black
and white — set perhaps
against the stars. At least
in your death there was
that beautiful woman tossing
that beautiful rose in the direction

of your grave. That child smiling
while adults wept the depth
of the ground. A certain eloquence
in the way the wind moved.

3.
So I look back to ninth grade when
I took Susan Dickerson
to our junior high prom, complete
with photographs and flowers and a shine
on the cafeteria linoleum. I'd learned
to dance by watching Fred Astaire
and Ginger Rogers glide around
the shrunken corners of the family T.V.
And I took Susan Dickerson, who would grow
to be lovely and blonde, a folksinger,
and I moved her elegant
around the floor where normally
the greasers ground their heels
into the tiles and spread
the crumbs of sandwiches they'd stolen
from the likes of me. I danced
Susan Dickerson, my first of dances,
until that melody ended and we moved
from the center of the floor to
where I smiled by the punch and cooled my soles
and she said, "Next time, you can lead."

4.
Our hero walks into the room.
There is a bed. A woman sits there.
The bedsheet rests at her waist.
She has the most perfect breasts
ever exposed in this century. In addition,
her smile is delightful. Naturally,
our hero has wandered into the wrong room.

5.

I spent several years trying to learn French
so that I could move beyond subtitles,
get by the middleman. But all I remember
are a few words — "monsieur," "beaucoup,"
and "merde" — and one sentence — "Que le vent
de ton cul se jette de ta bouche" — which translates
into "May the wind from your ass
trumpet through your mouth."

6.

I've tried to understand the French people
as well, wondering if they would make sense
only in your films. Tonight, for instance,
I watched a Jerry Lewis movie
because I know the French consider
him a genius. I turned off the sound
so that I could just watch him, not worry
about language. I let Schubert's
"Unfinished Symphony" play over
and over for two hours and I admit
I've never liked Jerry Lewis so much,
the buck teeth emerging andante
to the parting of his lips and the crossing
of his eyes.

7.

I saw *The Wild Child* in 1970.
It was in a theatre about a block
away from the General Motors Building.
A theatre that went broke eventually
from showing "art" movies and switched
to erotica. In *The Wild Child*
you played a doctor who had care
of a boy who grew up by himself
in the woods of France. In 1970,

I was growing up in the suburbs of Detroit.
As this boy discovered his humanity
he would sometimes go out
into the yard and scream
at the sky. You sat by the window
and watched him. You were not above
understanding what he was trying to say.

8.
These pictures come back to me:
I am on a bus from Memphis
to St. Paul. There is heavy snow.
I have the aisle seat next to this
big man dressed in torn, discolored clothes.
He gets up over twenty times
to use the bus bathroom.
All he says is "Gotta go again."
He keeps drinking water.
Once, he comes back
and he's pissed down his leg.
This is a bus with no seat free
except the one I'm in, next
to the man who's pissed down
his leg and is brushing up
against me every few miles
of this story. Finally, in St. Paul
I get away and find a locker
in the terminal so I can store
my luggage and walk away the tightness,
the smell of urine. But
when I open the locker
I find pornographic pictures—
two women, a blonde and a brunette
servicing the large cock
of a bored-looking Scandinavian.
Knowing I should throw them
away or at least ignore
them, I stuff the pictures

into one of my bags.
I will keep them for a while.

9.
On the bus from St. Paul to prairie
there are plenty of seats available. Yet
this mildly retarded boy from
Paynesville sits next to me,
and every time a woman
gets on the bus — in Buffalo,
in Eden Valley — he stands
and shouts to her, "Hey, ma'am,
you can sit here. Please,
take my seat." Each one refuses him
politely, but for all its emptiness,
his is the grand gesture
of my picaresque, that moment like
the lovers driving their car into a river
that will not entirely drown them.

10.
There is a man in the oriel
of the old house. He looks out
on the street, shouts through
the glass toward a woman
in some place on another side
of town. He knows she
will never hear him, but
every night he puts his voice
across the air; every night
the sound grows sweeter
and deeper than the night
before. He imagines she
has put an ear close to his mouth.

11.
Francois, I had a teacher once
who told me never to write letters

to the dead. Not only is it a morbid
habit, he said, it is also
a very difficult one to break.
He later told me never
to write love poems, nor use the word
"beauty," nor get up in the middle
of the night to jot down my dreams.
It is the middle of some night now
and here I am — as if sending
some letter home, with this montage
twisted into what I want to call
a beautiful rose that I let fall from
my fingertips toward you, with love.

Some Final Montana Songs

(for Richard Hugo)

1.

Even when the mines close
and their dust goes with them,
you can not keep away the children
with their torches. And you are never
so young in your bones as then.
You stand at what was an entrance once
to something dark and rich as
every Sally who ran her fingers
through your hair at 5 a.m. It seems
as though in time most every important
thing caves in or locks away
its light. Her hands were still
warm as she laughed. Even as she
smoothed the shadowy folds
of her dress. Even as you
like all the rest have closed
at last your eyes.

2.

Pesky as black flies the rumors.
You hold a grey lung in your left
hand. You're reasonably sure
that your right hand is empty.

3.

You take your woman down
to the fast stream. You fish
for trout or something else that
smells good frying in fat.

You drink beers with her. Talk
about who went crazy last week.
She throws her beer can, empty,
into these waters you've fished

for centuries. You figure
one can in a small river
won't make a goddamned bit
of difference. Still,

you wish she would've
tossed it on the bank
instead. Then a mouth nudges,
so delicately, your unbaited hook.

4.
Sometimes in the course of
your actual death you do not
die. Just an unlisted
number in Billings. A lost
address. A pale-mouthed woman
you don't like in a cheap
hotel with no detectives,
not even movies in the room.
A key that slipped through a hole
in your pocket and was picked
up by some young girl you'll never know.
There is always this young girl;
she is always picking up something
you've let slip. Always
you don't know anything
about her.

5.
This is how it ends. You're too drunk
to find anything but country
music on the radio. Your lover
left you for a miner and put
a pick axe on your bed so
you'll remember how it was.
She had scars shaped like fish

on her knees; she smoked Mexican
cigarettes; she hated poetry.
And you loved her. You will never
understand why she left you. You
have told that story before. This
was not the way it ended.

A Poem for My Students

Each poem says one thing: Love me or else.
Or else, love me.
—John Woods, from "At the Reading"

"Jesus," you think, "why us?"
as he unfolds the poem across a desk
and says, This is the table cloth
set for a fine banquet, but
you must bring the food; he says,
It is up to you whether
you taste beef Wellington or Spam.
He says. . . .
         It is Monday.
Every Monday he lays out these poems,
says they will make your lives
worthwhile. You are almost afraid
to tell him you are not unhappy.

JOHN REINHARD writes that "I was born in 1953 in Sault Ste. Marie, Michigan. And I later did time in various suburbs of Detroit. I did both undergraduate and graduate work at Eastern Michigan University. I came to Minnesota in 1983 and spent three years teaching at the University of Minnesota, Morris. Currently, I am an instructor at Winona State University." Reinhard was a recent winner of the Emerging Writers Competition of *Passages North* magazine, and he also won a Loft-McKnight Award in 1986.

I am particularly indebted to the following people for their contributions to the words and moments that become this book: Stephen Dunning (and his daughters), Laura Roop, Jill Moore, Oz Grobbel, Pamela Pierce, Jim Gremmels, William F. Petrik, Leona Mitchell Reinhard, Dr. Eugene Haun, Michael Moos, and Rebecca Colestock

photo by Sherida Bornfleth